What's the Difference Between an ALLIGATOR and a CROCODILE?

by Lisa Bullard ~ illustrated by Bandelin-Dacey

Picture Window Books
Minneapolis, Minnesota

For Joan, my strong, fearless, and long-standing friend

Thanks to our advisers for their expertise, research, and advice:

Michelle D. Boone, Ph.D., Assistant Professor
Department of Zoology
Miami University, Oxford, OH

Terry Flaherty, Ph.D., Professor of English
Minnesota State University, Mankato

Editor: Shelly Lyons
Designer: Abbey Fitzgerald
Page Production: Melissa Kes
Art Director: Nathan Gassman
Editorial Director: Nick Healy
Creative Director: Joe Ewest
The illustrations in this book were created with watercolor.

Photo Credits: Shutterstock/siloto (handmade paper), 1 and
22 (background) and throughout in sidebars and titlebars.

Picture Window Books
151 Good Counsel Drive
P.O. Box 669
Mankato, MN 56002-0669
877-845-8392
www.picturewindowbooks.com

Printed in the United States of America.

 All books published by Picture Window Books
are manufactured with paper containing at least
10 percent post-consumer waste.

Library of Congress Cataloging-in-Publication Data
Bullard, Lisa.
What's the difference between an alligator and a crocodile? / by Lisa Bullard ;
illustrated by Bandelin-Dacey.
p. cm. — (What's the difference?)
Includes index.
ISBN 978-1-4048-5547-2 (library binding)
1. Alligators—Juvenile literature. 2. Crocodiles—Juvenile
literature. I. Bandelin, Debra, ill. II. Dacey, Bob, ill. III. Title.
QL666.C925B86 2010
597.98—dc22   2009006887

Alligators and crocodiles first walked and swam on Earth during the time of the dinosaurs. The dinosaurs disappeared, but alligators and crocodiles remain.

Alligators and crocodiles have many things in common. But do you know the differences between an alligator and a crocodile?

3

It's easy to see why people get alligators and crocodiles confused. These two large reptiles look so much alike! Both animals have four short, strong legs. They have powerful tails to push them through the water. Their long snouts have many sharp teeth. And both animals are covered with rough, scaly skin that helps protect them. But most alligators have skin that looks darker than a crocodile's skin.

Alligators and crocodiles can live for a long time off the fat they store in their tails. Adults can go for months without eating.

alligator

crocodile

5

Both alligators and crocodiles are large animals. An American alligator is about 13 feet (4 meters) long. The largest alligators can weigh more than 1,000 pounds (450 kilograms).

American alligator

American crocodiles are usually about 15 feet (4.6 m) long. They can weigh as much as 2,000 pounds (900 kg).

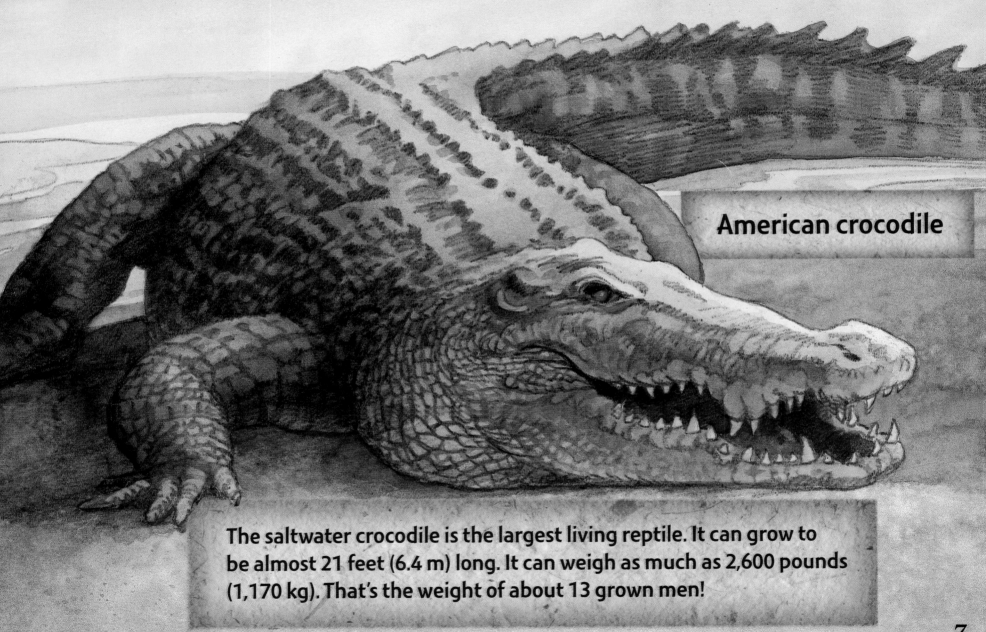

American crocodile

The saltwater crocodile is the largest living reptile. It can grow to be almost 21 feet (6.4 m) long. It can weigh as much as 2,600 pounds (1,170 kg). That's the weight of about 13 grown men!

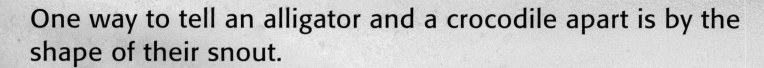

One way to tell an alligator and a crocodile apart is by the shape of their snout.

An alligator's snout is wide and rounded. It is shaped like the letter *U*.

8

Most crocodiles have a snout that is narrow and pointed. It is shaped like the letter *V*.

Use the alphabet to remember this difference. *Alligator* comes before *crocodile* in alphabetical order. The letter *U* also comes before *V* in the alphabet. An alligator's snout has the *U* shape.

Alligators and crocodiles have many teeth. But one tooth is larger and sticks up from the bottom jaw. This tooth is near the tip of the snout. When an alligator's mouth is closed, the tooth does not show. It fits into a pit inside the alligator's upper jaw.

Tooth is hidden

When a crocodile closes its mouth, you can see this large tooth sticking out from its bottom jaw.

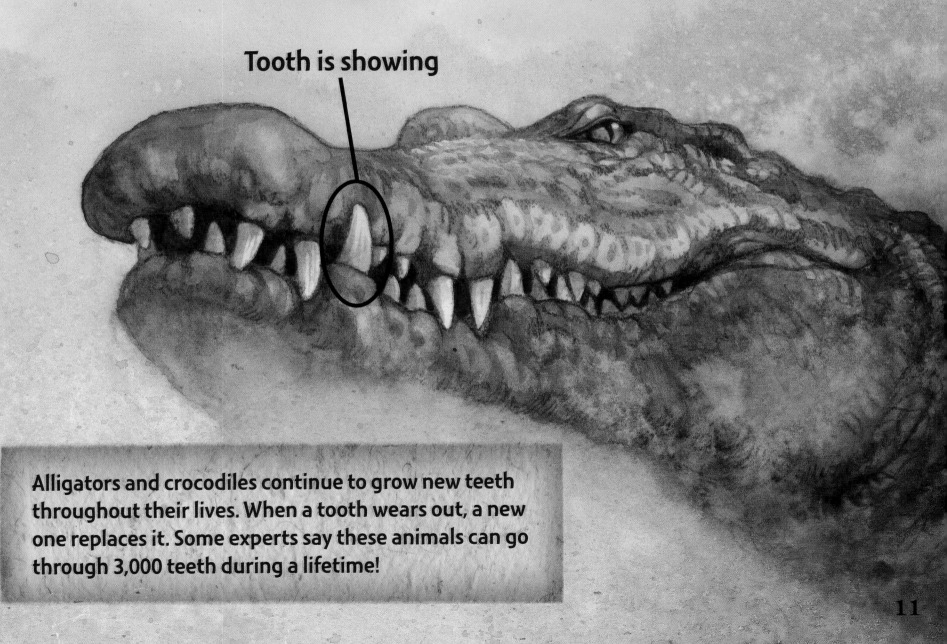

Tooth is showing

Alligators and crocodiles continue to grow new teeth throughout their lives. When a tooth wears out, a new one replaces it. Some experts say these animals can go through 3,000 teeth during a lifetime!

Alligators and crocodiles spend time on land and in water.

Alligators are excellent swimmers. They are usually found in freshwater bodies of water, such as swamps, rivers, and lakes.

Crocodiles are also excellent swimmers. They are found in fresh and salty water. Like alligators, they often lie in the water with only their nostrils, eyes, and back sticking out. By hiding most of their body underwater, they can take their prey by surprise.

Alligators and crocodiles eat meat. They eat small fish, reptiles, birds, and mammals.

There are only two kinds of alligators. The American alligator is found in parts of the southeastern United States. The Chinese alligator is very rare and now lives in only a small area of China.

American alligator

Chinese alligator

There are many different kinds of crocodiles. They are found in warm areas around the world.

Southern Florida is the only place where both crocodiles and alligators live close together in the wild.

Alligators and crocodiles are cold-blooded. That means their body temperature changes with their surroundings. They must warm themselves by lying in the sunlight. However, some alligators live in ponds and rivers where ice forms on the surfaces.

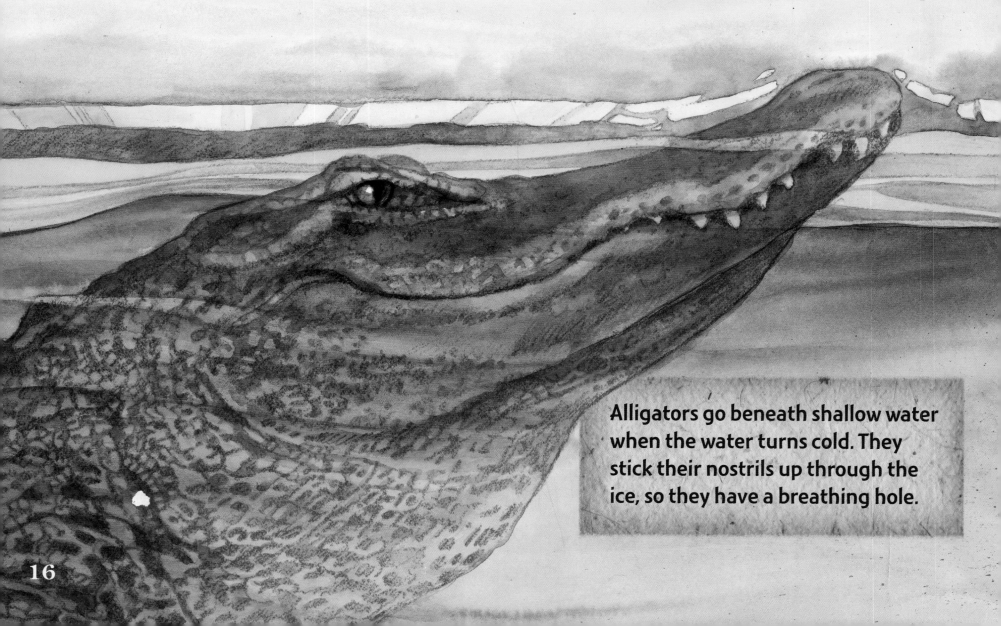

Alligators go beneath shallow water when the water turns cold. They stick their nostrils up through the ice, so they have a breathing hole.

Crocodiles live only in warm areas.

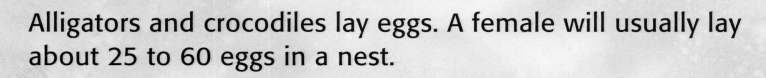

Alligators and crocodiles lay eggs. A female will usually lay about 25 to 60 eggs in a nest.

Female alligators build their nests on land. They make big mounds out of plants, twigs, and mud.

Some female crocodiles build mound nests, too. But others dig holes in the sand for their nests.

Both female crocodiles and alligators guard their nests. They are watchful mothers once their young hatch.

Alligator and crocodile eggs will develop into males or females depending upon the temperature at which the eggs are kept.

19

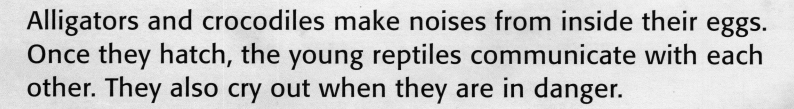

Alligators and crocodiles make noises from inside their eggs. Once they hatch, the young reptiles communicate with each other. They also cry out when they are in danger.

Adult alligators and crocodiles bellow, or roar. Male alligators make these noises to mark territory and attract females.

Male crocodiles also bellow to mark territory and attract females. But crocodiles are known to be much quieter than alligators.

Adult crocodiles and alligators use a form of communication called a head slap. They snap their jaws closed at water level. The movement makes a loud popping noise, followed by a splash.

21

ALLIGATOR

U-shaped snout

bottom tooth is hidden when mouth is closed

short, strong legs

rough, scaly, dark-colored skin

lives near freshwater

powerful tail

CROCODILE

powerful tail

V-shaped snout

bottom tooth is always visible

short, strong legs

rough, scaly, light-colored skin

lives near freshwater or saltwater

22

Fun Facts

Alligators and crocodiles have great power when they close their jaws. But the muscles that open their jaws are quite weak. People who are trained for it are able to keep the reptiles' jaws closed using just their hands.

Many alligators and crocodiles are considered an endangered or threatened species. Humans have often feared them, but not respected them. These animals are now protected by law.

Alligators and crocodiles often drag their prey into the water and drown it.

Alligators and crocodiles live an average of 30 to 70 years.

Alligators and crocodiles often stay underwater, not breathing, for several minutes. Studies show that they are able to stay underwater for up to two hours.

Alligators and crocodiles are about 3 inches (7.6 centimeters) long when they are born. Scientists believe the animals continue to grow throughout most of their lives

Glossary

cold-blooded—having a body temperature that changes with the surroundings

endangered—when an animal is one of the few of its kind left on Earth

mammals—animals that have a backbone, have hair or fur, feed their young milk, are warm-blooded, and have lungs that take in oxygen

nostrils—two holes at the end of a nose, used for breathing

prey—animals that are hunted and eaten for food

reptiles—animals that have a backbone, have scales, are cold-blooded, have lungs, and (usually) lay eggs

scaly—covered in small pieces of tough skin

snout—an animal's long nose

species—a specific kind of animal with certain characteristics

territory—the land or water area in which an animal raises its young and grazes or hunts for food

To Learn More

More Books to Read

Dennard, Deborah. *Alligators and Crocodiles*. Chanhassen, Minn.: NorthWord Press, 2003.

Landau, Elaine. *Alligators and Crocodiles: Hunters of the Night*. Berkeley Heights, N.J.: Enslow Elementary, 2008.

Trueit, Trudi Strain. *Alligators and Crocodiles*. New York: Children's Press, 2003.

Internet Sites

FactHound offers a safe, fun way to find Internet sites related to this book. All of the sites on FactHound have been researched by our staff.

Here's all you do:

Visit *www.facthound.com*

FactHound will fetch the best sites for you!

Index

American alligator, 14
American crocodile, 7
bellowing, 20, 21
Chinese alligator, 14
cold-blooded, 16
eggs, 18, 19
food, 13
head slap, 21
homes, 12, 13, 14, 15, 16, 17, 22
jaws, 23
legs, 4, 22
length, 6, 7, 23
lifespan, 23
nests, 18, 19
saltwater crocodile, 7
skin, 4, 22
snouts, 4, 8, 9, 22
southern Florida, 15
tails, 4, 22
teeth, 4, 10, 11, 22
weight, 6, 7

Look for all of the books in the What's the Difference? series:

What's the Difference Between a Butterfly and a Moth?

What's the Difference Between a Frog and a Toad?

What's the Difference Between a Leopard and a Cheetah?

What's the Difference Between an Alligator and a Crocodile?